GW00771074

The Spiritual Meaning of Advent & Christmas

Homilies and Addresses for
Advent & Christmas

by
Benedict XVI

All booklets are published thanks to the
generous support of the members of the
Catholic Truth Society

CATHOLIC TRUTH SOCIETY
PUBLISHERS TO THE HOLY SEE

Contents

Advent 3

Walking in a New Beginning .3

Christ's Glorious Return 8

Spiritual Meaning of Christmas 12

Unique Christmas Atmosphere of Grace 19

The Christmas Tree 20

Christmas 21

God in the Stable 21

Under the Blessed Gaze of Mary 29

New Year - Pray for Grace and Peace 35

God's Manifestation at the Epiphany 42

I am here, I know you, I love you 50

ADVENT

Walking in a New Beginning

We begin the itinerary of a new liturgical year, entering into the first of its seasons: Advent. In the First Letter to the Thessalonians, the Apostle Paul uses precisely this word: "coming", which in Greek is *Parousia* and *adventus* in Latin (1 *Thes* 5:23). According to the common tradition of this text, Paul urges the Christians of Thessalonica to keep themselves blameless "*for* the coming" of the Lord. However, in the original text one reads "*in* the coming" (εν τη παρουσια), almost as if the advent of the Lord were more than a future point in time but rather a spiritual place in which to walk already in the present, while waiting, and in which one is indeed perfectly preserved in every personal dimension. In fact, it is exactly this that we live out in the liturgy. By celebrating the liturgical seasons we actualize the mystery in this case the Lord's coming as it were "walking in it" towards its full realization at the end of time, but already drawing sanctifying virtue from it, since the last times have already begun with Christ's death and Resurrection.

A season of hope

The word that sums up this particular state, in which one
awaits something that is to be manifested but of which
one also already has a glimpse and a foretaste, is "hope".
Advent is the spiritual season of hope *par excellence*, and
in it the whole Church is called to become hope, for
herself and for the world. The whole organism of the
Mystical Body acquires, so to speak, the "colour" of
hope. The whole People of God continue on their journey,
attracted by this mystery: that our God is "the God who
comes" and calls us to go to meet him. How? In the first
place in that universal form of hope and expectation
which is prayer, which is eminently expressed in the
Psalms, human words in which God himself has placed
and continually places the invocation of his coming on
the lips and in the hearts of believers. Let us therefore
reflect for a few moments on two of his Psalms which we
have just prayed and which are consecutive in the biblical
Book: Psalms 141 and 142, according to the Jewish
numbering.

Prayer and spiritual offering

"I have called to you, Lord; make haste to help me! / Hear
my voice, when I cry to you. / Let my prayer arise before
you like incense, / the raising of my hands like an evening
oblation" (*Ps* 141[140]:1-2). Thus begins the first Psalm

of the First Vespers for the first week of the Psalter: words which, at the beginning of Advent, acquire a new "colour", because the Holy Spirit makes them resound ever anew within us in the Church on her way between the time of God and human times. "Lord, hasten to help me!" It is the cry of someone who feels he is in grave danger but it is also the cry of the Church amid the many threats that surround her, that threaten her holiness, the irreproachable integrity of which the Apostle Paul speaks which instead must be preserved for the Lord's coming. And in this invocation the cry of all the just also resounds, of all those who want to resist evil, the seduction of an iniquitous well-being, of pleasures offensive to human dignity and to the condition of the poor. At the beginning of Advent the Church's liturgy once again makes this cry her own, and raises it to God "like incense" (v. 2). The evening offering of incense is in fact a symbol of prayer, of the outpouring of hearts turned to God, to the Most High, as well as "the raising of... hands like an evening oblation" (v. 2). Material sacrifices, as it also took place in the Jewish temple, are no longer offered in the Church, but the spiritual offering of prayer is raised, joined to that of Jesus Christ who is at the same time Sacrifice and Priest of the new and eternal covenant. In the cry of the Mystical Body we recognize the very voice of the Head: the Son of God who has taken upon himself our trials and our temptations, to give us the grace of his victory.

This identification of Christ with the Psalmist is particularly evident in the second Psalm (142). Here, every word, every invocation, makes one think of Jesus in his Passion, and in particular of his prayer to the Father in Gethsemane. In his first coming, with the Incarnation, the Son of God wanted to share fully in our human condition. Of course, he did not share in sin, but for our salvation suffered all its consequences. In praying Psalm 142 the Church relives every time the grace of this compassion, of this "coming" of the Son of God in human anguish so deeply as to plumb its depths. The Advent cry of hope then expresses from the outset and very powerfully, the full gravity of our state, of our extreme need of salvation. It is as if to say: we await the Lord not in the same way as a beautiful decoration upon a world already saved, but as the only way of liberation from a mortal danger and we know that he himself, the Liberator, had to suffer and die to bring us out of this prison (cf. v. 8).

Paschal Hope

In short, these two Psalms shelter us from any temptation to escape or flee from reality; they preserve us from a false hope that might desire to enter Advent and move towards Christmas forgetting the tragedy of our personal and collective existence. In fact, a trustworthy hope that is not deceptive, can only be a "Paschal" hope, as the canticle of the Letter to the Philippians reminds us every

Saturday evening, with which we praise the Incarnate Christ, crucified, Risen and our universal Lord. Let us turn our gaze and our heart to him, in spiritual union with the Virgin Mary, Our Lady of Advent. Let us place our hand in hers and enter joyfully into this new time of grace that God gives as a gift to his Church for the good of all humanity. Like Mary and with her maternal help, let us make ourselves docile to the action of the Holy Spirit, so that the God of peace may sanctify us totally, and the Church become a sign and instrument of hope for all men. Amen.

Christ's Glorious Return

On the First Sunday of Advent, we enter that four-week Season with which a new liturgical year begins and that immediately prepares us for the Feast of Christmas, the memorial of the Incarnation of Christ in history. Yet, the spiritual message of Advent is more profound and already orients us to the glorious return of the Lord at the end of our history. Adventus is the Latin word that could be translated by "arrival", "coming" or "presence". In the language of the ancient world it was a technical term that indicated the arrival of an official, and especially the visit of kings or emperors to the provinces, but it could also be used for the appearance of a divinity, which emerged from its hidden dwelling-place and thus manifested its divine power; its presence was solemnly celebrated with worship.

The visit of the King

By using this term, "Advent", Christians wanted to express the special relationship that bound them to the Crucified and Risen Christ. He is a King who, having entered this poor province called Earth, made us the gift of his visit and after his Resurrection and Ascension into Heaven desired in any case to stay with us; we perceive his mysterious presence in the liturgical assembly. Indeed, in celebrating the Eucharist, we proclaim that he did not withdraw from the world, that he did not leave us alone and, even though we cannot see and touch him as with material and tangible realities, he is in any case with us and among us. Indeed, he is in us, because he can attract to himself and communicate his life to every believer who opens his/her heart to him. Thus, Advent means commemorating the first coming of the Lord in the flesh, with his definitive return already in mind, and, at the same time, it means recognizing that Christ present in our midst makes himself our travelling companion in the life of the Church who celebrates his mystery. This knowledge, dear brothers and sisters, nourished by listening to the Word of God, must help us to see the world with different eyes, to interpret the individual events of life and history as words that God addresses to us, as signs of his love that assure us of his closeness in every situation; this awareness, in particular, should prepare us to welcome him when "he will come again in glory to judge the living and the dead and his kingdom will have no end", as in a little while we shall repeat in the Creed. In this perspective, Advent becomes for all Christians a time of expectation and hope, a privileged time for listening and reflection, as long as we let ourselves be guided by the liturgy, which invites us to advance to meet the Lord who comes.

"Come, Lord Jesus"

"Come, Lord Jesus": dear friends, this ardent invocation of the Christian community of the early days must also become our constant aspiration, the aspiration of the Church in every epoch, which longs for and prepares herself for the encounter with her Lord. Come today, Lord; enlighten us, give us peace, help us triumph over violence. Come Lord, we pray precisely in these weeks: "Lord... let us see your face and will shall be saved" (*Ps* 80[79]:3), we have just prayed with the words of the Responsorial Psalm. And the Prophet Isaiah revealed to us in the First Reading that the Face of Our Saviour is that of a tender and merciful father who cares for us in all circumstances because we are the work of his hands: "You, O Lord, are our Father, our Redeemer from of old is your name" (63:16). Our God is a father prepared to forgive repentant sinners and to welcome those who trust in his mercy (cf. *Is* 64:4). We had drifted away from him because of sin, falling under the dominion of death, but he took pity on us and, on his own initiative, without any merit on our part, decided to meet our needs, sending his only Son as our Redeemer. As we face such a great mystery of love, our thanksgiving rises spontaneously and our invocation becomes more trusting: Show us your steadfast love, O Lord, today, in our time, in every part of the world, let us feel your presence and grant us your salvation.

Going to meet Christ like St Lawrence

At the beginning of Advent what better message can we glean from St Lawrence than that of holiness? He repeats to us that holiness, that is, going to meet Christ who comes ceaselessly to visit us, does not go out of fashion, on the contrary as time passes it shines brightly and expresses the perennial striving for God of humankind.

To help prepare ourselves for Christ's coming is also the exhortation we hear in the Gospel: "Watch", Jesus tells us in Luke's short parable about the master of the house who goes on a journey but the date of whose return is unknown (cf. *Mk* 13:33-37). Watching means following the Lord, choosing what Christ chose, loving what he loved, conforming one's own life to his; watching means passing every instant of our time in the sphere of his love without letting oneself be disheartened by the inevitable difficulties and problems of daily life. This is what St Lawrence did, this is what we must do and let us ask the Lord to grant us his grace so that Advent may be an incentive for all to walk in this direction. May Mary, the humble Virgin of Nazareth chosen by God to become Mother of the Redeemer, St Andrew, and St Lawrence, an example of fearless Christian faithfulness to the point of martyrdom, guide us and go with us. Amen!

Spiritual Meaning of Christmas

The days of Advent that directly prepare us for the Nativity of the Lord begin: we are in the *Christmas Novena* which in many Christian communities is celebrated with liturgies rich in biblical texts, all oriented to fostering the expectation of the Saviour's Birth. Indeed, the whole Church focuses her gaze of faith on this Feast that is now at hand, preparing herself, as she does every year, to join in the joyful singing of the Angels who will announce to the shepherds in the heart of the night the extraordinary event of the Birth of the Redeemer, inviting them to go to the Grotto in Bethlehem. It is there that the Emmanuel lies, the Creator who made himself a creature, wrapped in swaddling clothes and lying in a poor manger (cf. *Lk* 2:13-16).

A universal celebration

Because of the atmosphere that distinguishes it, Christmas is a universal celebration. In fact, even those who do not profess themselves to be believers can perceive in this annual Christian event something extraordinary and transcendent, something intimate that speaks to the heart. It is a Feast that praises the gift of life. The birth of a child must always be an event that brings joy; the embrace of a newborn baby usually inspires feelings of kindness and care, of emotion and tenderness. Christmas is the encounter with a newborn baby lying in a humble grotto. In contemplating him in the manger, how can we fail to think of all those children who continue to be born today in great poverty in many regions of the world? How can we fail to think of those newborn infants who are not welcomed, who are rejected, who do not manage to survive because of the lack of care and attention? How can we fail to think also of the families who long for the joy of a child and do not see their hope fulfilled? Unfortunately, under the influence of hedonist consumerism, Christmas risks losing its spiritual meaning and being reduced to a mere commercial opportunity for purchases and the exchange of gifts! However, it is true that the difficulties, the uncertainties and the financial crisis itself that numerous families have had to come to terms with in recent months and which is affecting all humanity could be an incentive to rediscover the warmth of simplicity, friendship and solidarity: typical values of Christmas. Stripped of its consumerist and materialistic encrustations, Christmas can thus become an opportunity for welcoming, as a personal gift, the message of hope that emanates from the mystery of Christ's Birth.

A Commemoration of our salvation

However, none of this enables us to fully grasp the ineffable value of the Feast for which we are preparing. We know that it celebrates the central event of history: the Incarnation of the divine Word for the redemption of humanity. In one of his many Christmas Homilies, St Leo the Great exclaims: "Let us be glad in the Lord, dearly-beloved, and rejoice with spiritual joy that there has dawned for us the day of ever-new redemption, of ancient preparation, of eternal bliss. For as the year rolls round, there recurs for us the commemoration of our salvation, which promised from the beginning, accomplished in the fullness of time will endure for ever" (*Homily* XXII). St Paul returns several times in his Letters to this fundamental truth. For example, he writes to the Galatians: "When the time had fully come, God sent forth his Son, born of woman, born under the law... so that we might receive adoption as sons" (4:4). In the Letter to the Romans he highlights the logic and the demanding consequences of this salvific event: "If we are children of God... then [we are] heirs, heirs of God and fellow heirs with Christ, provided we suffer with him in order that we may also be glorified with him" (8:17). However, in the Prologue to the fourth Gospel, it is above all St John who meditates profoundly on the mystery of the Incarnation. And it is for this reason that the Prologue has been part of the Christmas liturgy since the very earliest times.

Indeed, in it are found the most authentic expression and the most profound synthesis of this Feast and of the basis of its joy. St John writes: "*Et Verbum caro factum est et habitavit in nobis* / and the Word became flesh and dwelt among us" (*Jn* 1:14).

Celebrating the incarnation

At Christmas, therefore, we do not limit ourselves to commemorating the birth of a great figure: we do not simply and abstractly celebrate the birth of the man or in general the mystery of life; even less do we celebrate only the beginning of the new season. At Christmas we commemorate something very tangible and important for mankind, something essential for the Christian faith, a truth that St John sums up in these few words: "*The Word became flesh*". This was a historical event that the Evangelist Luke was concerned to situate in a well-defined context: in the days when the decree was issued for the first census of Caesar Augustus, when Quirinius was Governor of Syria (cf. *Lk* 2:1-7). Therefore, it was on a historically dated night that the event of salvation occurred for which Israel had been waiting for centuries. In the darkness of the night of Bethlehem a great light really was lit: the Creator of the universe became flesh, uniting himself indissolubly with human nature so as truly to be "God from God, Light from Light" yet at the same time a man, true man. What John calls in Greek "*ho logos*" translated into Latin as "*Verbum*" and Italian as "il Verbo" also means "the Meaning". Thus we can understand John's words as: the "eternal Meaning" of the world made himself tangible to our senses and our minds: we may now touch him and contemplate him (cf. 1 *Jn* 1:1). The "Meaning" that became flesh is not merely a general idea inherent in the world; it is a "Word" addressed to us. The *Logos* knows us, calls us, guides us. The Word is not a universal law within which we play some role, but rather a Person who is concerned with every individual person: he is the Son of the living God who became man in Bethlehem.

A meaning exists

To many people, and in a certain way to all of us, this seems too beautiful to be true. In fact, here it is reaffirmed to us: yes, a meaning exists, and the meaning is not a powerless protest against the absurd. The meaning has power: it is God. A good God who must not be confused with any sublime and remote being, whom it would never be possible to reach, but a God who made himself our neighbour and who is very close to us, who has time for each one of us and who came to stay with us. It then comes naturally to ask ourselves: "However could such a thing be possible? Is it dignified for God to make himself a child?". If we are to seek to open our hearts to this truth that illuminates the whole of human existence we must bend our minds and recognize the limitations of our intelligence. In the Grotto of Bethlehem God shows himself to us as a humble "infant" to defeat our arrogance. Perhaps we would have submitted more easily to power and wisdom, but he does not want us to submit; rather, he appeals to our hearts and to our free decision to accept his love. He made himself tiny to set us free from that human claim to grandeur that results from pride. He became flesh freely in order to set us truly free, free to love him.

The value of existence and a time of conversion

Christmas is a privileged opportunity to meditate on the meaning and value of our existence. The approach of this Solemnity helps us on the one hand to reflect on the drama of history in which people, injured by sin, are perennially in search of happiness and of a fulfilling sense of life and death; and on the other, it urges us to meditate on the merciful kindness of God who came to man to communicate to him directly the Truth that saves, and to enable him to partake in his friendship and his life. Therefore let us prepare ourselves for Christmas with humility and simplicity, making ourselves ready to receive as a gift the light, joy and peace that shine from this mystery. Let us welcome the Nativity of Christ as an event that can renew our lives today. The encounter with the Child Jesus makes us people who do not think only of

themselves but open themselves to the expectations and
needs of their brothers and sisters. In this way we too will
become witnesses of the radiance of Christmas that
shines on the humanity of the third millennium. Let us
ask Mary Most Holy, Tabernacle of the Incarnate Word,
and St Joseph, the silent witness of the events of
salvation, to communicate to us what they felt while they
were waiting for the Birth of Jesus, so that we may
prepare ourselves to celebrate with holiness the
approaching Christmas, in the joy of faith and inspired by
the commitment to sincere conversion.

Unique Christmas Atmosphere of Grace

The Nativity of the Lord is at hand. Every family feels the desire to come together to enjoy the special, unique atmosphere that this holy day is able to bring about... I like to think of it as a kind of prolongation of that mysterious joy, that deep exultation that enveloped the Holy Family, the angels and the shepherds of Bethlehem on the night of Jesus' birth. I would describe it as an "atmosphere of grace", recalling Saint Paul's words in the Letter to Titus: "*Apparuit gratia Dei Salvatoris nostri omnibus hominibus*" (cf. *Tit* 2:11).

The Apostle says that the grace of God has appeared "for all". I would say that this also reveals the mission of the Church and, in particular, that of the Successor of Peter and his collaborators: to help make the grace of God, the Redeemer, ever more visible to everyone and to bring salvation to all.

The Christmas Tree

In the coming weeks, the Christmas tree will be a cause of joy for many. From my study window I too shall be able to look out joyfully again and again, when from above I will be able to admire anew the tree and manger. But there will also be the chance for me to go to it directly, praying before the Baby Jesus and rejoicing for the light of the tree and for its beauty. Its towering shape, its green colour and the lights decorating its branches are symbols of life. In addition, it refers us to the mystery of the Holy Night. Christ, the Son of God brings to the dark, cold and unredeemed world into which he is born a new hope and a new splendour. If man lets himself be moved and enlightened by the splendour of the living truth that is Christ, he will feel inner peace in his heart and will become a peacemaker in a society that so longs for reconciliation and redemption.

CHRISTMAS

God in the Stable

"Who is like the Lord our God, who is seated on high, who looks far down upon the heavens and the earth?" This is what Israel sings in one of the Psalms (113 [112], 5ff.), praising God's grandeur as well as his loving closeness to humanity. God dwells on high, yet he stoops down to us... God is infinitely great, and far, far above us. This is our first experience of him. The distance seems infinite. The Creator of the universe, the one who guides all things, is very far from us: or so he seems at the beginning. But then comes the surprising realization: The One who has no equal, who "is seated on high", looks down upon us. He stoops down. He sees us, and he sees me. God's looking down is much more than simply seeing from above. God's looking is active. The fact that he sees me, that he looks at me, transforms me and the world around me. The Psalm tells us this in the following verse: "He raises the poor from the dust..." In looking down, he raises me up, he takes me gently by the hand and helps me – me! – to rise from depths towards the heights. "God stoops down". This is a prophetic word. That night in

Bethlehem, it took on a completely new meaning. God's stooping down became real in a way previously inconceivable. He stoops down – he himself comes down as a child to the lowly stable, the symbol of all humanity's neediness and forsakenness. God truly comes down. He becomes a child and puts himself in the state of complete dependence typical of a newborn child. The Creator who holds all things in his hands, on whom we all depend, makes himself small and in need of human love. God is in the stable. In the Old Testament the Temple was considered almost as God's footstool; the sacred ark was the place in which he was mysteriously present in the midst of men and women. Above the temple, hidden, stood the cloud of God's glory. Now it stands above the stable. God is in the cloud of the poverty of a homeless child: an impenetrable cloud, and yet – a cloud of glory! How, indeed, could his love for humanity, his solicitude for us, have appeared greater and more pure? The cloud of hiddenness, the cloud of the poverty of a child totally in need of love, is at the same time the cloud of glory. For nothing can be more sublime, nothing greater than the love which thus stoops down, descends, becomes dependent. The glory of the true God becomes visible when the eyes of our hearts are opened before the stable of Bethlehem.

God revealed himself to the Lowly

Saint Luke's account of the Christmas story tells us that God first raised the veil of his hiddenness to people of very lowly status, people who were looked down upon by society at large – to shepherds looking after their flocks in the fields around Bethlehem. Luke tells us that they were "keeping watch". This phrase reminds us of a central theme of Jesus's message, which insistently bids us to keep watch, even to the Agony in the Garden – the command to stay awake, to recognize the Lord's coming, and to be prepared. Here too the expression seems to imply more than simply being physically awake during the night hour. The shepherds were truly "watchful" people, with a lively sense of God and of his closeness. They were waiting for God, and were not resigned to his apparent remoteness from their everyday lives. To a watchful heart, the news of great joy can be proclaimed: for you this night the Saviour is born. Only a watchful heart is able to believe the message. Only a watchful heart can instill the courage to set out to find God in the form of a baby in a stable. Let us now ask the Lord to help us, too, to become a "watchful" people.

Surrounded by God's glory

Saint Luke tells us, moreover, that the shepherds themselves were "surrounded" by the glory of God, by the

cloud of light. They found themselves caught up in the
glory that shone around them. Enveloped by the holy
cloud, they heard the angels' song of praise: "Glory to God
in the highest heavens and peace on earth to people of his
good will". And who are these people of his good will if
not the poor, the watchful, the expectant, those who hope
in God's goodness and seek him, looking to him from afar?

Joyful amazement at God's love

The Fathers of the Church offer a remarkable
commentary on the song that the angels sang to greet the
Redeemer. Until that moment – the Fathers say – the
angels had known God in the grandeur of the universe, in
the reason and the beauty of the cosmos that come from
him and are a reflection of him. They had heard, so to
speak, creation's silent song of praise and had
transformed it into celestial music. But now something
new had happened, something that astounded them. The
One of whom the universe speaks, the God who sustains
all things and bears them in his hands – he himself had
entered into human history, he had become someone who
acts and suffers within history. From the joyful
amazement that this unimaginable event called forth,
from God's new and further way of making himself
known – say the Fathers – a new song was born, one
verse of which the Christmas Gospel has preserved for
us: "Glory to God in the highest heavens and peace to his

people on earth". We might say that, following the structure of Hebrew poetry, the two halves of this double verse say essentially the same thing, but from a different perspective. God's glory is in the highest heavens, but his high state is now found in the stable – what was lowly has now become sublime. God's glory is on the earth, it is the glory of humility and love. And even more: the glory of God is peace. Wherever he is, there is peace. He is present wherever human beings do not attempt, apart from him, and even violently, to turn earth into heaven. He is with those of watchful hearts; with the humble and those who meet him at the level of his own "height", the height of humility and love. To these people he gives his peace, so that through them, peace can enter this world.

The medieval theologian William of Saint Thierry once said that God – from the time of Adam – saw that his grandeur provoked resistance in man, that we felt limited in our own being and threatened in our freedom. Therefore God chose a new way. He became a child. He made himself dependent and weak, in need of our love. Now – this God who has become a child says to us – you can no longer fear me, you can only love me.

God became a child for our sake

With these thoughts, we draw near this night to the child of Bethlehem – to the God who for our sake chose to become a child. In every child we see something of the

Child of Bethlehem. Every child asks for our love. This night, then, let us think especially of those children who are denied the love of their parents. Let us think of those street children who do not have the blessing of a family home, of those children who are brutally exploited as soldiers and made instruments of violence, instead of messengers of reconciliation and peace. Let us think of those children who are victims of the industry of pornography and every other appalling form of abuse, and thus are traumatized in the depths of their soul. The Child of Bethlehem summons us once again to do everything in our power to put an end to the suffering of these children; to do everything possible to make the light of Bethlehem touch the heart of every man and woman. Only through the conversion of hearts, only through a change in the depths of our hearts can the cause of all this evil be overcome, only thus can the power of the evil one be defeated. Only if people change will the world change; and in order to change, people need the light that comes from God, the light which so unexpectedly entered into our night.

Praying for peace in Bethlehem

And speaking of the Child of Bethlehem, let us think also of the place named Bethlehem, of the land in which Jesus lived, and which he loved so deeply. And let us pray that peace will be established there, that hatred and violence will cease. Let us pray for mutual understanding, that hearts will be opened, so that borders can be opened. Let us pray that peace will descend there, the peace of which the angels sang that night.

The trees of the forest acclaim him

In Psalm 96 [95], Israel, and the Church, praises God's grandeur manifested in creation. All creatures are called to join in this song of praise, and so the Psalm also contains the invitation: "Let all the trees of the wood sing for joy before the Lord, for he comes" (v. 12ff.). The Church reads this Psalm as a prophecy and also as a task. The coming of God to Bethlehem took place in silence. Only the shepherds keeping watch were, for a moment, surrounded by the light-filled radiance of his presence and could listen to something of that new song, born of the wonder and joy of the angels at God's coming. This silent coming of God's glory continues throughout the centuries. Wherever there is faith, wherever his word is proclaimed and heard, there God gathers people together and gives himself to them in his Body; he makes them his Body. God "comes". And in this way our hearts are awakened. The new song of the angels becomes the song of all those who, throughout the centuries, sing ever anew of God's coming as a child – and rejoice deep in their hearts. And the trees of the wood go out to him and exult. The tree in Saint Peter's Square speaks of him, it wants to reflect his splendour and to say: Yes, he has come, and the trees of the wood acclaim him. The trees in the cities and in our homes should be something more than a festive custom: they point to the One who is the reason for our joy – the God who comes, the God who for our sake became a child. In the end, this song of praise, at the deepest level, speaks of him who is the very tree of new-found life. Through faith in him we receive life. In the Sacrament of the Eucharist he gives himself to us – he gives us a life that reaches into eternity. At this hour we join in creation's song of praise, and our praise is at the same time a prayer: Yes, Lord, help us to see something of the splendour of your glory. And grant peace on earth. Make us men and women of your peace. Amen.

Under the Blessed Gaze of Mary

"*O admirabile commercium!* O marvellous exchange!".
Thus begins the Antiphon of the first Psalm [of first
vespers for the feast of Mary Mother of God], to then
continue: "man's Creator has become man, born of a
virgin". "By your miraculous birth of the Virgin you have
fulfilled the Scriptures", proclaims the Antiphon of the
Second Psalm, which is echoed by the words of the third
Antiphon that introduce us to the canticle taken from the
Letter of Paul to the Ephesians: "Your blessed and fruitful
virginity is like the bush, flaming yet unburned, which
Moses saw on Sinai. Pray for us, Mother of God". Mary's
divine motherhood is also highlighted in the brief
Reading proclaimed shortly beforehand, which proposes
anew the well-known verses of the Letter to the
Galatians: "When the designated time had come, God
sent forth his Son, born of woman... so that we might
receive our status as adopted sons" (*Gal* 4:4-5). And
again, in the traditional *Te Deum* that we will raise at the
end of our celebration before the Most Holy Sacrament
solemnly exposed for our adoration singing, "*Tu, ad
liberandum suscepturus hominem, non horruisti Virginis
uterum*", in English: "when you, O Christ, became man to
set us free you did not spurn the Virgin's womb".

Mary – truly the Mother of God

Thus everything invites us to turn our gaze to the one who "received the Word of God in her heart and in her body and gave Life to the world", and for this very reason the Second Vatican Ecumenical Council recalls "is acknowledged and honoured as being truly the Mother of God" (*Lumen gentium*, n. 53). Christ's Nativity, which we are commemorating in these days, is entirely suffused with the light of Mary and, while we pause at the manger to contemplate the Child, our gaze cannot fail to turn in gratitude also to his Mother, who with her "yes" made possible the gift of Redemption. This is why the Christmas Season brings with it a profoundly Marian connotation; the birth of Jesus as God and man and Mary's divine motherhood are inseparable realities; the mystery of Mary and the mystery of the Only-Begotten Son of God who was made man form a single mystery, in which the one helps to better understand the other.

Mary Mother of God, *Theotokos, Dei Genetrix*. Since ancient times Our Lady has been honoured with this title. However, for many centuries in the West there was no feast specifically dedicated to the divine Motherhood of Mary. It was introduced into the Latin Church by Pope Pius XI in 1931 on the occasion of the 15th centenary of the Council of Ephesus, and he chose to establish it on 11 October. On that date, in 1962, the Second Vatican Council was inaugurated. It was then the Servant of God Paul VI who restored an ancient tradition in 1969, fixing this Solemnity on 1 January. In the Apostolic Exhortation *Marialis cultus* of 2 February 1974, he explained the reason for his decision and its connection with the World Day of Peace. "In the revised ordering of the Christmas period it seems to us that the attention of all should be directed towards the restored Solemnity of Mary the holy Mother of God," Paul VI wrote. "This celebration... is meant to commemorate the part played by Mary in this mystery of salvation. It is meant also to exalt the singular dignity which this mystery brings to the "holy Mother'.... It is likewise a fitting occasion for renewing adoration to the newborn Prince of Peace, for listening once more to the glad tidings of the angels (cf. *Lk* 2:14), and for imploring from God, through the Queen of Peace, the supreme gift of peace" (n. 5).

A time for thanksgiving and penance

Let us place in the hands of the heavenly Mother of God our choral hymn of thanksgiving to the Lord for the gifts he has generously granted us during the past 12 months. The first sentiment which spontaneously rises in our hearts this evening is precisely that of praise and thanksgiving to the One who gave us time, a precious opportunity to do good; let us combine with it our request for forgiveness for perhaps not always having spent it usefully... By coming into the world, the eternal Word of the Father revealed to us God's closeness and the ultimate truth about man and his eternal destiny; he came to stay with us to be our irreplaceable support, especially in the inevitable daily difficulties. And this evening the Virgin herself reminds us of what a great gift Jesus gave us with his Birth, of what a precious "treasure" his Incarnation constitutes for us. In his Nativity Jesus comes to offer us his Word as a lamp to guide our steps; he comes to offer us himself and we must always affirm him as our unfailing hope in our daily life, aware that "it is only in the mystery of the Word made flesh that the mystery of man truly becomes clear" (*Gaudium et spes*, n. 22).

Sharing the gift of Christ's presence

Christ's presence is a gift that we must be able to share with everyone... This is why we as believers can also make a great contribution to overcoming the current educational emergency. Thus, for a profound evangelization and a courageous human promotion that can communicate the riches that derive from the encounter with Christ to as many people as possible, an increase in synergy among families, school and parishes is more important than ever...

In our times, marked by uncertainty and concern for the future, it is necessary to experience the living presence of Christ. It is Mary, Star of Hope who leads us to him. It is she, with her maternal love, who can guide young people especially who bear in their hearts an irrepressible question about the meaning of human existence to Jesus. I know that various groups of parents, meeting in order to deepen their vocation, are seeking new ways to help their children respond to the big existential questions. I cordially urge them, together with the whole Christian community, to bear witness to the new generations of the joy that stems from encountering Jesus, who was born in Bethlehem and did not come to take something from us but rather to give us everything.

To young people

On Christmas night I had a special thought for children; instead, this evening it is young people above all on whom I wish to focus my attention. Dear young people, responsible for the future of this our city, do not be afraid of the apostolic task that the Lord is entrusting to you. Do not hesitate to choose a lifestyle that does not follow the current hedonistic mindset. The Holy Spirit assures you of the strength you need to witness to the joy of faith and the beauty of being Christian. The growing need for evangelization requires many labourers in the Lord's vineyard; do not hesitate to respond to him promptly if he calls you. Society needs citizens who are not concerned solely with their own interests because, as I recalled on Christmas Day, "If people look only to their own interests, our world will certainly fall apart".

We shall never hope in vain

The year is ending with an awareness of the spreading social and financial crisis that now involves the whole world; a crisis that asks for greater moderation and solidarity from all, so that they may go to the aid especially of the individuals and families who are in the most serious difficulty. The Christian community is already making efforts toward this and I know that the diocesan *Caritas* and other relief agencies are doing their utmost. Nonetheless, everyone's collaboration is necessary, for no one can think of building his own happiness alone. Although many clouds are gathering on the horizon of our future, we must not be afraid. Our great hope as believers is eternal life in communion with Christ and the whole family of God. This great hope gives us the strength to face and to overcome the difficulties of life in this world. This evening the motherly presence of Mary assures us that God never abandons us if we entrust ourselves to him and follow his teachings. Therefore, while we take our leave of 2008 and prepare to welcome 2009, let us present to Mary our expectations and hopes, as well as our fears and the difficulties that dwell in our hearts, with filial affection and trust. She, the Virgin Mother, offers us the Child who lies in the manger as our sure hope. Full of trust, we shall then be able to sing at the end of the *Te Deum*: "*In te, Domine, speravi: non confundar in aeternum* - In you, Lord, is our hope: and we shall never hope in vain". Yes, Lord, in you we hope, today and for ever; you are our hope. Amen!

New Year - Pray for Grace and Peace

On the first day of the year, divine Providence brings us together for a celebration that moves us each time because of the riches and beauty of its correspondence: the civil New Year converges with the culmination of the Octave of Christmas on which the divine Motherhood of Mary is celebrated, and this gathering is summed up felicitously in the World Day of Peace. In the light of Christ's Nativity, I am pleased to address my best wishes to each one for the year that has just begun... My good wishes echo the good wishes that the Lord himself addresses to us in the liturgy of the Word. A Word which, starting with the event in Bethlehem, recalled in its historical actuality by the Gospel of Luke (2:16-21) and reinterpreted in all its saving importance by the Apostle Paul (*Gal* 4:4-7), becomes a Blessing for the People of God and for all humanity.

Thus the ancient Jewish tradition of blessing is brought to completion (*Nm* 6:22-27): the priests of Israel blessed the people by putting the Lord's Name upon them: "so shall they put my name upon the people of Israel". With a triple formula present in the First Reading the sacred Name was invoked upon the faithful three times, as a wish for grace and peace. This remote custom brings us back to an essential reality: to be able to walk on the way of peace, men and women and peoples need to be illumined by the "Face" of God and to be blessed by his "Name". Precisely this came about definitively with the Incarnation: the coming of the Son of God in our flesh and in history brought an irrevocable blessing, a light that is never to be extinguished and offers believers and people of good-will alike the possibility of building the civilization of love and peace.

Christ's grace brings a peaceful revolution

The Second Vatican Council said in this regard that "by his Incarnation, he, the Son of God, has in a certain way united himself with each man" (*Gaudium et spes*, n. 22). This union confirms the original design of a humanity created in the "image and likeness" of God. In fact, the Incarnate Word is the one, perfect and consubstantial image of the invisible God. Jesus Christ is the perfect man. "Human nature", the Council reaffirms: "by the very fact that it was assumed... in him, has been raised in us also to a dignity beyond compare" (*ibid.*). For this reason the earthly history of Jesus that culminated in the Paschal Mystery is the beginning of a new world, because he truly inaugurated a new humanity, ever and only with Christ's grace, capable of bringing about a peaceful "revolution". This revolution was not an ideological but spiritual revolution, not utopian but real, and for this reason in need of infinite patience, sometimes of very long periods, avoiding any short cuts and taking the hardest path: the path of the development of responsibility in consciences.

God chose poverty

...The Birth of Jesus in Bethlehem reveals to us that God chose poverty for himself in coming among us. The scene that the shepherds were the first to see and that confirmed the angel's announcement to them, was a stable in which Mary and Joseph had found shelter, and a manger in which the Virgin had laid the newborn Child wrapped in swaddling clothes (cf. *Lk* 2:7, 12, 16). *God chose this poverty*. He wanted to be born thus but we can immediately add: he wanted to live and also to die in this condition. Why? St Alphonsus Maria Liguori explains it in a Christmas carol that is known all over Italy: "You, Creator of the world had no clothes, no fire, O my Lord. My dear Divine Child, how I love this poverty, since for love you made yourself poorer still". This is the answer: love for us impelled Jesus not only to make himself man, but also to make himself poor. Along these same lines we can quote St Paul's words in the Second Letter to the Corinthians: "For you are well acquainted", he writes, with "the favour shown you by our Lord Jesus Christ: how for your sake he made himself poor though he was rich, so that you might become rich by his poverty" (8:9). St Francis of Assisi was an exemplary witness of this poverty chosen for love. The Franciscan charism, in the history of the Church and of Christian civilization, constitutes a widespread trend of evangelical poverty which has done and continues to do such great good for the Church and for the human family. Returning to St Paul's wonderful synthesis on Jesus, it is significant also for our reflection today that it was inspired in the Apostle precisely while he was urging the Christians of Corinth to be generous in collecting money for the poor. He explains: "I do not mean that others should be eased and you burdened, but that as a matter of equality your abundance at the present time should supply their want" (2 *Cor* 8:13).

We must fight deprivation

This is a crucial point... there is a poverty, a deprivation, which God does not desire and which should be "fought" as the theme of this World Day of Peace says; a poverty that prevents people and families from living as befits their dignity; a poverty that offends justice and equality and that, as such, threatens peaceful co-existence. This negative acceptation also includes all the non-material forms of poverty that are also to be found in the rich and developed societies: marginalization, relational, moral and spiritual poverty...

Thus it is necessary to seek to establish a "virtuous circle" between the poverty "to be chosen" and the poverty "to be fought". This gives access to a path rich in fruits for humanity's present and future and which could be summarized thus: to fight the evil poverty that oppresses so many men and women and threatens the peace of all, it is necessary to rediscover moderation and solidarity as evangelical, and at the same time universal, values. More practically, it is impossible to combat poverty effectively unless one does what St Paul wrote to the Corinthians, in other words if one does not seek "to create equality", reducing the gap between those who waste the superfluous and those who lack what they need. This entails just and sober decisions, which are moreover made obligatory by the need to administer the earth's limited resources wisely. When he says that Jesus Christ "for [our] sake became poor", St Paul offers an important indication not only from the theological point of view but also at the sociological level; not in the sense that poverty is a value in itself, but because it is a condition that demonstrates solidarity. When Francis of Assisi stripped himself of his possessions, it was a decision to witness that was inspired in him directly by God, but at the same time it shows everyone the way of trust in Providence. Thus, in the Church, the vow of poverty is the commitment of some, but it reminds all of the need to be detached from material goods and of the

primacy of spiritual riches. This is therefore the message
for us today: the poverty of Christ's Birth in Bethlehem,
as well as being the subject of adoration for Christians, is
also a school of life for every man. It teaches us that to
fight both material and spiritual poverty, the path to take
is the path of solidarity that impelled Jesus to share our
human condition.

The mystery of the poverty of God
understood by Mary

I believe that the Virgin Mary must have asked herself
this question several times: why did Jesus choose to be
born of a simple, humble girl like me? And then, why did
he want to come into the world in a stable and have his
first visit from the shepherds of Bethlehem? Mary
received her answer in full at the end, having laid in the
tomb the Body of Jesus, dead and wrapped in a linen
shroud (cf. *Lk* 23:53). She must then have fully
understood the mystery of the poverty of God. She
understood that God made himself poor for our sake, to
enrich us with his poverty full of love, to urge us to
impede the insatiable greed that sparks conflicts and
divisions, to invite us to moderate the mania to possess
and thus to be open to reciprocal sharing and acceptance.
Let us trustingly address to Mary, Mother of the Son of
God who made himself our brother, our prayer that she
will help us follow in his footsteps, to fight and overcome

poverty, to build true peace, which is *opus iustitiae*. Let us entrust to her the profound desire to live in peace that wells up in the hearts of the vast majority of the Israeli and Palestinian peoples, once again jeopardized by the outbreak of violence on a massive scale in the Gaza Strip, in response to other violent incidents. Even violence, even hatred and distrust are forms of poverty perhaps the most appalling "to fight". May they not get the upper hand! In this regard the Pastors of those Churches, in these distressing days, have made their voices heard. Together with them and their beloved faithful, especially those of the small but fervent parish of Gaza, let us place at Mary's feet our anxieties for the present and our fears for the future, and likewise the well-founded hope that with the wise and far-sighted contribution of all it will not be impossible to listen to one another, to come to one another's help and to give concrete responses to the widespread aspiration to live in peace, safety and dignity. Let us say to Mary: accompany us, heavenly Mother of the Redeemer, throughout the year that begins today, and obtain from God the gift of peace for the Holy Land and for all humanity. Holy Mother of God, pray for us. Amen.

God's Manifestation at the Epiphany

Epiphany, the "manifestation" of Our Lord Jesus Christ, is a many-facetted mystery. The Latin tradition identifies it with the visit of the Magi to the Infant Jesus in Bethlehem and thus interprets it above all as a revelation of the Messiah of Israel to the Gentiles. The Eastern tradition on the other hand gives priority to the moment of Jesus' Baptism in the River Jordan when he manifested himself as the Only-Begotten Son of the heavenly Father, consecrated by the Holy Spirit. John's Gospel, however, also invites us to consider as an "epiphany" the Wedding at Cana, during which, by changing the water into wine, Jesus "manifested his glory; and his disciples believed in him" (*Jn* 2:11). And what should we say, dear brothers and sisters, especially we priests of the New Covenant who are every day witnesses and ministers of the "epiphany" of Jesus Christ in the Holy Eucharist? The Church celebrates all the mysteries of the Lord in this most holy and most humble Sacrament in which he both reveals and conceals his glory. "*Adoro te devote, latens Deitas*" in adoration, thus we pray along with St Thomas Aquinas.

The Magi

...In all likelihood the Wise Men were astronomers. From their observation point, situated in the East compared to Palestine, perhaps in Mesopotamia, they had noticed the appearance of a new star and had interpreted this celestial phenomenon as the announcement of the birth of a king, specifically that in accordance with the Sacred Scriptures of the King of the Jews (cf. *Nm* 24:17). The Fathers of the Church also saw this unique episode recounted by St Matthew as a sort of cosmic "revolution" caused by the Son of God's entry into the world. For example, St John Chrysostom writes: "The star, when it stood over the young Child, stayed its course again: which thing itself was of a greater power than belongs to a star, now to hide itself, now to appear, and having appeared to stand still" (*Homily on the Gospel of Matthew*, 7, 3). St Gregory of Nazianzen states that the birth of Christ gave the stars new orbits (cf. *Dogmatic Poems* v. 53-64: *PG* 37, 428-429). This is clearly to be understood in a symbolic and theological sense. In effect, while pagan theology divinized the elements and forces of the cosmos, the Christian faith, in bringing the biblical Revelation to fulfilment, contemplates only one God, Creator and Lord of the whole universe.

Divine love

The divine and universal law of creation is divine love, incarnate in Christ. However, this should not be understood in a poetic but in a real sense. Moreover, this is what Dante himself meant when, in the sublime verse that concludes the Paradiso and the entire *Divina Commedia*, he describes God as "the Love which moves the sun and the other stars" (*Paradiso*, xxxiii, 145). This means that the stars, planets and the whole universe are not governed by a blind force, they do not obey the dynamics of matter alone. Therefore, it is not the cosmic elements that should be divinized. Indeed, on the contrary, within everything and at the same time above everything there is a personal will, the Spirit of God, who in Christ has revealed himself as Love (cf. Encyclical *Spe Salvi*, 5). If this is the case, then as St Paul wrote to the Colossians people are not slaves of the "elemental spirits of the universe" (cf. *Col* 2:8) but are free, that is, capable of relating to the creative freedom of God. God is at the origin of all things and governs all things, not as a cold and anonymous engine but rather as Father, Husband, Friend, Brother and as the *Logos*, "Word-Reason" who was united with our mortal flesh once and for all and fully shared our condition, showing the superabundant power of his grace. Thus there is a special concept of the cosmos in Christianity which found its loftiest expression in medieval philosophy and theology. In our day too, it shows interesting signs of a new flourishing, thanks to the enthusiasm and faith of many scientists who following in Galileo's footsteps renounce neither reason nor faith; instead they develop both in their reciprocal fruitfulness.

Christian thought compares the cosmos to a "book", Galileo said this as well considering it as the work of an Author who expresses himself in the "symphony" of the Creation. In this symphony is found, at a certain point, what might be called in musical terminology a "solo", a theme given to a single instrument or voice; and it is so important that the significance of the entire work depends on it. This "solo" is Jesus, who is accompanied by a royal sign: the appearance of a new star in the firmament. Jesus is compared by ancient Christian writers to a new sun. According to current astrophysical knowledge, we should compare it with a star that is even more central, not only for the solar system but also for the entire known universe. Within this mysterious design simultaneously physical and metaphysical, which led to the appearance of the human being as the crowning of Creation's elements Jesus came into the world: "born of woman" (*Gal* 4:4), as St Paul writes. The Son of man himself epitomizes the earth and Heaven, the Creation and the Creator, the flesh and the Spirit. He is the centre of the cosmos and of history, for in him the Author and his work are united without being confused with each other.

No shadow can obscure Christ's light

In the earthly Jesus the culmination of Creation and of history is found but in the Risen Christ this is surpassed: the passage through death to eternal life anticipates the point of the "recapitulation" of all things in Christ (cf. *Eph* 1:10). Indeed "all things", the Apostle wrote "were created through him and for him" (*Col* 1:16). And it is precisely with the resurrection of the dead that he became "pre-eminent in all things" (*Col* 1:18). Jesus himself affirms this, appearing to his disciples after the Resurrection: "all authority in Heaven and on earth has been given to me" (*Mt* 28:18). This awareness supports the way of the Church, Body of Christ, on the paths of history. There is no shadow, however dark, that can obscure Christ's light. This is why believers in Christ never lack hope, even today, in the face of the great social and financial crisis that is tormenting humanity, in the face of the destructive hatred and violence that have not ceased to stain many of the earth's regions with blood, in the face of the selfishness and pretension of the human being in establishing himself as his own God, which sometimes leads to dangerous distortions of the divine plan concerning life and the dignity of the human being, the family and the harmony of the Creation. Our efforts to free human life and the world from the forms of poison and contamination that could destroy the present and the future retain their value and meaning as I noted in the Encyclical *Spe Salvi* mentioned above even if we apparently fail or seem powerless when hostile forces appear to gain the upper hand, because "it is the great hope based upon God's promises that gives us courage and directs our action in good times and bad" (n. 35).

Christ's universal lordship is exercised in a special way
on the Church. We read in the Letter to the Ephesians that
God "has put all things under [Christ's] feet and has made
him the head over all things for the Church, which is his
body, the fullness of him who fills all in all" (*Eph* 1:22-23).
The Epiphany is the manifestation of the Lord and as a
reflection, it is the manifestation of the Church, since the
Body is inseparable from the Head. Today's First Reading,
from "Third Isaiah", gives us the precise perspective for
understanding the reality of the Church as a mystery of
reflected light: "Arise, shine" the Prophet says, addressing
Jerusalem, "for your light has come, / and the glory of the
Lord has risen upon you" (*Is* 60:1). The Church is
humanity illuminated, "baptized" in the glory of God, that
is in his love, in his beauty, in his dignity. The Church
knows that her own humanity, with its limitations and
wretchedness, serves especially to highlight the work of
the Holy Spirit. She can boast of nothing, save in her Lord.
It is not from her that light comes; the glory is not hers. But
this is precisely her joy, which no one can take from her: to
be a "sign and instrument" of the One who is "*lumen
gentium*", the light of humanity (cf. Second Vatican
Council, Dogmatic Constitution *Lumen gentium*, n. 1).

We are servants of the Word

The Feast of the Epiphany invites the Church, and in her,
every community and every individual member of the

faithful, to imitate, as did the Apostle to the Gentiles, the service that the star rendered to the Magi from the East, guiding them to Jesus (cf. St Leo the Great, *Disc. 3 for Epiphany*, 5: *PL* 54, 244). What was Paul's life after his conversion other than a "race" to bring the light of Christ to the peoples, and vice versa, to lead the peoples to Christ? God's grace made Paul a "star" for the Gentiles. His ministry is an example and an incentive for the Church to rediscover herself as essentially missionary and to renew the commitment to proclaim the Gospel, especially to those who do not yet know it. Yet, in looking at St Paul, we cannot forget that his preaching was completely nourished by the Sacred Scriptures. Therefore it should be powerfully reaffirmed in the perspective of the recent Assembly of the Synod of Bishops that the Church and individual Christians can be a light that leads to Christ only if they are diligently and intimately nourished by the Word of God. It is the Word, certainly not us, that illumines, purifies and converts. We are merely servants of the Word of life. This is how Paul saw himself and his ministry: as a service to the Gospel. "I do it all for the sake of the Gospel", he wrote (1 *Cor* 9: 23). The Church, every ecclesial community, every Bishop and every priest ought also to be able to say this: "I do it all for the sake of the Gospel". Dear brothers and sisters, pray for us, Pastors of the Church, that by assimilating the Word of God daily we may pass it on faithfully to our brethren. Yet we too pray for you, all the faithful, because every Christian is called through Baptism and Confirmation to proclaim Christ, the light of the world, in word and in the witness of his life. May the Virgin Mary, Star of Evangelization, help us to bring this mission to completion together, and may St Paul, the Apostle to the Gentiles, intercede for us from Heaven. Amen.

I am here, I know you, I love you

The words that the Evangelist Mark recounts at the beginning of his Gospel: "You are my beloved Son; with you I am well pleased" (1:11), introduce us into the heart of today's Feast of the Baptism of the Lord with which the Christmas Season ends. The cycle of the Christmas Solemnities leads us to meditate on the birth of Jesus, announced by the angels who were surrounded with the luminous splendour of God; the Christmas Season speaks to us of the star that guided the Magi of the East to the House in Bethlehem, and invites us to look to Heaven, which opens above the Jordan as God's voice resounds. These are all signs through which the Lord never tires of repeating: "Yes, I am here. I know you. I love you. There is a path that leads from me to you. And there is a path that rises from you to me". The Creator assumed the dimensions of a child in Jesus, of a human being like us, to make himself visible and tangible. At the same time, by making himself small, God caused the light of his greatness to shine. For precisely by lowering himself to the point of defenceless vulnerability of love, he shows what his true greatness is indeed, what it means to be God.

Baptism introduces us into a personal relationship with Jesus

Christmas, and more generally the liturgical year, is exactly that drawing near to these divine signs, to recognize them as impressed into daily events, so that our hearts may be open to God's love. And if Christmas and Epiphany serve primarily to render us capable of seeing, of opening our eyes and hearts to the mystery of a God who comes to be with us, then we can say that the Feast of the Baptism of Jesus introduces us into the daily regularity of a personal relationship with him. Indeed, by immersion in the waters of the Jordan, Jesus united himself with us. Baptism is, so to speak, the bridge he built between himself and us, the road on which he makes himself accessible to us. It is the divine rainbow over our lives, the promise of God's great "yes", the door of hope and, at the same time, the sign that that indicates to us the path to take actively and joyfully in order to encounter him and feel loved by him.

The heavens are truly open and continue to open

I am truly glad that this year too, on this Feast day, I have been granted the opportunity to baptize these children. God's "favour" rests on them today. Ever since the Only-Begotten Son of the Father had himself baptized, the heavens are truly open and continue to open, and we may entrust every new life that begins into the hands of the

One who is more powerful than the dark powers of evil. This effectively includes Baptism: we restore to God what came from him. The child is not the property of the parents but is entrusted to their responsibility by the Creator, freely and in a way that is ever new, in order that they may help him or her to be a free child of God. Only if the parents develop this awareness will they succeed in finding the proper balance between the claim that their children are at their disposal, as though they were a private possession, shaping them on the basis of their own ideas and desires, and the libertarian approach that is expressed in letting them grow in full autonomy, satisfying their every desire and aspiration, deeming this the right way to cultivate their personality. If, with this sacrament, the newly-baptized becomes an adoptive child of God, the object of God's infinite love that safeguards him and protects him from the dark forces of the evil one, it is necessary to teach the child to recognize God as Father and to be able to relate to him with a filial attitude. And therefore, when in accordance with the Christian tradition as we are doing today children are baptized and introduced into the light of God and of his teachings, no violence is done to them. Rather, they are given the riches of divine life in which is rooted the true freedom that belongs to the children of God a freedom that must be educated and modelled as the years pass to render it capable of responsible personal decisions.

A baptism that saves

Returning now to the Gospel passage, let us seek to better understand what is happening today. St Mark recounts that it was just when John the Baptist was preaching on the banks of the River Jordan, proclaiming the urgent need for conversion in view of the now imminent coming of the Messiah, that Jesus, who was among the crowds, presented himself to be baptized. John's Baptism is indisputably a Baptism of penance, very different from the sacrament that Jesus was to institute. At that moment, however, the Redeemer's mission is already glimpsed because, when he comes out of the water, a voice comes from Heaven and the Holy Spirit descends upon him (cf. *Mk* 1:10); the heavenly Father proclaims him as his beloved Son and publicly attests to his universal saving mission, which will be fully accomplished with his death on the Cross and his Resurrection. Only then, with the Paschal Sacrifice, would the forgiveness of sins be rendered universal and total. With Baptism we do not simply emerge from the waters of the Jordan to proclaim our commitment to conversion, but the redeeming Blood of Christ that purifies and saves us is poured out upon us. It is the Father's beloved Son, in whom he was pleased, who regains for us the dignity and joy of calling ourselves truly "children" of God.

54

We relive this mystery evoked by today's solemnity; the signs and symbols of the sacrament of Baptism help us to understand what the Lord works in the hearts of these our little ones, making them "his" for ever, the chosen dwelling place of his Spirit and "living stones" for the construction of the spiritual temple which is the Church. May the Virgin Mary, Mother of Jesus, the beloved Son of God, watch over them and their families and always accompany them, so that they may fully carry out the plan of salvation that is brought into their lives through Baptism. And may we, dear brothers and sisters, accompany them with our prayers. Let us pray for parents, godparents, godfathers and godmothers and for their relatives, so that they may help them grow in faith. Let us pray for all of us so that, by devoutly taking part in this celebration, we may renew the promises of our Baptism and give thanks to the Lord for his constant assistance. Amen!

Sources

This booklet draws together homilies and addresses of Pope Benedict XVI made over the period December 2008 to January 2009, during Advent and Christmastide:

Walking in a New Beginning - Homily of His Holiness Pope Benedict XVI at the Celebration of First Vespers of the First Sunday of Advent, St Peter's Basilica, Saturday, 29 November 2008

Christ's Glorious Return - Homily of His Holiness Pope Benedict XVI on the occasion of his pastoral visit to the Basilica of Saint Lawrence Outside the Walls on the occasion of the 1750th anniversary of the martyrdom of the holy deacon, First Sunday of Advent, 30 November 2008

Spiritual Meaning of Christmas - Pope Benedict XVI, General Audience, Paul VI Audience Hall Wednesday, 17 December 2008

Unique Christmas Atmosphere of Grace - Address of His Holiness Benedict XVI to the Members Of The Roman Curia for the Traditional Exchange of Christmas Greetings, Clementine Hall, Monday, 22 December 2008

The Christmas Tree - Address of His Holiness Benedict XVI to Pilgrims from Lower Austria who had come to bring as a gift to the Holy Father the Christmas Tree which will decorate St Peter's Square in the Christmas Season, Hall of Blessings, Friday, 12 December 2008

God in the Stable - Homily of His Holiness Benedict XVI, Midnight Mass, Solemnity of the Nativity of the Lord, Saint Peter's Basilica, Thursday, 25 December 2008

Under the Blessed Gaze of Mary - Homily of His Holiness Benedict XVI, Te Deum and First Vespers of the Solemnity of Mary, Mother of God, St Peter's Basilica, Wednesday, 31 December 2008

New Year - Pray for Grace and Peace - Homily of His Holiness Benedict XVI, Solemnity of Mary, Mother of God and 42nd World Day of Peace, St Peter's Basilica, Thursday, 1st January 2009

God's Manifestation at the Epiphany - Homily of His Holiness Benedict XVI, Eucharistic Celebration on the Solemnity of the Epiphany of the Lord, St Peter's Basilica, Tuesday, 6 January 2009

I am here, I know you, I love you - Homily of His Holiness Benedict XVI, Mass in the Sistine Chapel and Administration of the Sacrament of Baptism, Feast of the Baptism of the Lord, Sunday, 11 January 2009